THE

CONSTITUTIONAL POWERS

OF THE

GENERAL CONFERENCE,

WITH A SPECIAL APPLICATION TO THE SUBJECT OF

SLAVEHOLDING.

BY

WILLIAM L. HARRIS.

CINCINNATI:
PRINTED AT THE METHODIST BOOK CONCERN.
R. P. THOMPSON, PRINTER.

1860.

PREFACE.

At the General conference held in Indianapolis in 1856 a proposition was made by the Committee on Slavery to insert a new chapter on that subject in the Discipline. Its provisions, though more stringent than any existing rule on the subject, did not propose to make *all* slaveholding a disqualification for membership, but they did in effect propose to make the fact that a man *is* a slaveholder *prima facie* evidence of his unfitness for a place in the Church, and to put upon him the labor and duty of showing, to the satisfaction of a committee before whom he should be held to answer, such a set of attending circumstances as would, in their estimation, justify the "*merely legal relation*" for the time, and, with a view to ultimate and speedy emancipation, requiring the master meanwhile to render to the slave that which is *just* and *equal*, and to *treat him properly*.

This proposition met with a very determined opposition from a portion of the members of the General conference who styled themselves "CONSERVATIVES" *par excellence*, and whose rallying cry on the subject of slavery was, "THE DISCIPLINE AS IT IS."

The ostensible ground of hostility to the proposed measure was the alleged *unconstitutionality* of the new chapter. 1. It was alleged to be in *conflict* with the existing General Rule on slavery. One of the most distinguished members of the last General conference said: "*This test can not go into the book* *without the alteration of the General Rule on that subject. Leaving that untouched you put into the book a statute that conflicts directly with the Rule and with all rational interpretation of it.*"* Another said of "the Discipline as it is" that "*the existing General Rule* AUTHORIZES *simple slaveholding*," and then added: "*Let it come out, sir, for the sake of frankness, for the sake of repentance, for the sake of amendment, let it be acknowledged that, historically,* CONSTITUTIONALLY, *administratively, we have been a* SLAVEHOLDING, *though an antislavery Church.*" Of the proposed chapter he said: It "*violates*"—"*contravenes*"—"*interferes with*"—is "*incompatible with*"—is "*in contravention of*" the existing General Rule on slavery.† 2.

* Daily Western Christian Advocate, May 28, 1856.
† Daily Western Christian Advocate, May 30, 1856.

The proposed new chapter was resisted on the ground that it instituted a new term of membership in the Church. It was, indeed, declared that so much of the chapter as "provides for giving them [the slaves] 'such compensation as shall be just and equal,' and for their proper treatment, made a *new* test of membership;" and for the reason, as was alleged, that such provisions could not be met without changing "*entirely the relation of master and slave,*" and making "*the slave a free man.*"* And again it was argued that the proposed chapter was "*a double assault upon the constitution of the Church,*" because, in proposing "*to make non-slaveholding a term of membership,*" it "*violates not only the existing General Rule, which prohibits only the 'buying and selling'*

* Daily Western Christian Advocate, May 28, 1856.

of slaves, but also the 'Restrictive,' by rejecting the only authorized process to such a change."*

These declarations were put forth by leading men of the opposition in the last General conference, and, so far as appeared in the discussions, such doctrines were held in common by most if not all who opposed the introduction of a new chapter into the Discipline. For these ministers personally I entertained the highest regard, but I believed honestly that they and others had entirely misapprehended the *import* of the General Rule on slavery, as well as the *scope* of the fourth restriction upon the powers of the General conference. To both these points I have given some attention in the following argument. I have studiously avoided all discussion

* Daily Western Christian Advocate, May 30, 1856.

relating to either the *propriety* or *expediency* of a rule excluding slaveholders from the Church, neither have I considered the policy of any *proposed measure* for securing such a rule if it were deemed best to make it. I have chosen rather to confine myself strictly to the question as to the *power* of the General conference to make such a rule. This question has presented itself to me as involving principles susceptible of indefinite application and vital to the interests of the Church. In this I may be mistaken, but so it has seemed to me. It relates exclusively to the prerogatives of the supreme council of the Church, and its examination ought not to be incumbered with extraneous matters of policy or expediency. That the General conference is competent to pass a simple rule of Discipline which will exclude all slaveholders from the Church, I have not the shadow of a doubt; but if this assumption be true, it concludes nothing as to what particular *measures* will be most promotive of the peace, purity, and prosperity of the Church.

If in the course of the argument I have advocated any erroneous opinions, the obvious remedy is to refute them. I am utterly unconscious of having made use of a fallacy, or of having misconstrued or misapplied authorities, or of having substituted declamation for argument; but if any such defects exist it is easy to point them out.

When I wrote the articles, the substance of which is given in the following pages, it was not my expectation that they would have any thing more than a merely ephemeral newspaper existence. Soon after their publication I received letters from many ministers, some of whom occupy high positions in the Church, fully indorsing my doctrines, and calling for the argument in a more permanent form. The *Delaware annual conference,* of which I have the honor to be a member, at its session in 1858 *unanimously* adopted the following resolution; namely,

> "*Resolved,* That we fully indorse the views of Dr. Harris in his argument on the constitutional powers of the General conference as published in the Western Christian Advocate, and that this conference respectfully request him to publish his articles in a more permanent form."

The same conference at its session in 1859, with the same unanimity, passed the following resolution; namely,

> "*Resolved,* That we again request Dr. Harris to publish his argument on the constitu-

tional powers of the General conference in a more permanent form."

Not feeling at liberty longer to decline meeting the wishes of my own conference, and of so many friends of the ministry in other conferences, I have amplified the articles somewhat, for the purpose of noticing objections which have been made to my doctrines since they were first published; and, foregoing my own preferences and yielding to the solicitations of others, I now send them forth in this unpretending little volume, asking only that it be read and its arguments refuted before its doctrines be condemned.

WILLIAM L. HARRIS.

OHIO WESLEYAN UNIVERSITY,
Delaware, Ohio, January 2, 1860.

CONTENTS.

INTRODUCTION.

PAGE.

Statement of the Question ... 15

CHAPTER I.

Powers granted to a delegated General Conference ... 21

CHAPTER II.

Does the Constitution of the Church forbid the General Conference to make a Rule prohibiting Slaveholding in the Church? ... 41

CHAPTER III.

Does the General Rule on Slavery authorize Slaveholding? ... 49

CHAPTER IV.

General Rules and Terms of Membership ... 66

CHAPTER V.

Recapitulation of the Argument and Authorities ... 130

CHAPTER VI.

Perils of the Membership ... 151

THE GENERAL CONFERENCE AND SLAVERY.

INTRODUCTION.

IS THE GENERAL CONFERENCE COMPETENT TO PASS A SIMPLE RULE OF DISCIPLINE WHICH WILL EXCLUDE ALL SLAVEHOLDERS FROM THE CHURCH?

The discussion of this question involves no controversy either in relation to the necessity or expediency of such an exscinding rule, or concerning the policy of any given measure to secure its enactment. What are the powers of the General conference, and what will be a wise and discreet use of these powers, are questions totally distinct. It can never be expedient for the General conference to *transcend* its powers. It may be equally inexpedient to do some things for which its powers are ample. It can abrogate every thing in the book of Discipline save the Articles of Religion and the Restrictive and General Rules; and yet such action would be considered highly inexpedient and improper. And were it settled beyond all cavil that the General conference has full authority to pass a rule excluding all slaveholders from the Church, it does not follow of necessity that such a rule ought to be made. It might still be an open question whether such a rule is desirable, and, if desirable, whether considerations of policy and expediency should not induce the General conference to forbear such legislation, and allow slaveholders to remain in the Church till an extirpatory rule can be enacted by the Restrictive Rule process. These questions are entitled to careful and prayerful consideration. But whatever conclusions may be reached concerning the issues they involve, these conclusions in no way affect the subject under examination; for it relates simply and exclusively to the constitutional prerogatives of the supreme council of the Church. In relation to an exscinding statutory rule there are two questions to be considered: first, *Has the General conference authority to make it?* Second, *is it just and proper that it should make it?* The first question should be first determined; for if the General conference has no authority to make such a rule, that fact of itself carries with it an emphatic negative of

2

the second question, for it can never be expedient to violate law unless law violates justice. Leaving all questions of expediency to others, this argument will be confined strictly to the topic of conference authority.

The provisions of the constitution of the Church bearing on this question relate to what, for the want of a better term, will be denominated the *legislative** powers of the General conference. The provisions comprise three things:

1. *A grant of powers.* The grant is

---

* By "*legislative powers*" is meant simply the power to make rules and regulations "*for our Church,*" as specified in the grant, and it is used here in no broader sense. Those *rules and regulations* must be pertinent to the ends and aims of a Church organization. The General conference exercises, therefore, no *civil* legislation. In relation to the *moral* code, it is not the prerogative of the General conference to *add to,* to *take from, to alter,* or *to modify* a single item of the *Divine law;* but it is its prerogative to declare what the Gospel requires in relation to a given subject, and

made in these words: *The General conference shall have full powers to make rules and regulations for our Church under the following limitations and restrictions.*

2. Six rules defining these limitations and restrictions.

3. *The "General Rules of the United Societies,"* of which the fourth Restrictive Rule is conservative.

Any modification of the Restrictive Rules, or any revocation or change of the "General Rules," can be lawfully secured only by the concurrent action

---

then by disciplinary rules to enforce that requirement. As Christ prescribed no form of Church government or organization, it is the right and duty of the General conference, subject to constitutional restrictions, to prescribe such rules of Church *order* and polity as it may deem necessary to the efficiency and perpetuity of the Church. As Christ left a *moral* code, the conference follows him in that; as Christ left no *ecclesiastical* code, the conference enacts such as it deems best.

of the General and annual conferences, as provided for in the sixth Restrictive Rule. It will be seen that the General conference has, by express constitutional grant, power to make rules and regulations for the Church, subject, however, to a code or body of articles, six in number, which are called *Restrictive Rules, or Articles.* In other words, the General conference has legislative powers conferred on it by a constitution restricting and limiting its powers.

In discussing the question proposed it will, therefore, be proper to consider,

1. The powers given to the General conference as they are defined by the terms of the grant; and,

2. The restrictions imposed on the use of the powers granted.

CHAPTER I.

SCOPE OF THE POWERS GRANTED.

WHAT *are the powers given to the General conference by the terms of the grant?* The constitution of the Church differs essentially in the powers it delegates, from our state and federal constitutions. In these latter all powers not expressly granted to the government are reserved to the people, or to the states, while in the former all powers not expressly reserved or excepted are delegated to the General conference. It has been so held by the highest judicial tribunal of the Church* as

* "Reply to the Protest," Journal of General Conference of 1844, pages 203, 204.

well as by the Supreme Court of the nation.*

The constitution gives to the General conference *full powers* to make rules and regulations under defined limitations—power to make *all* rules and regulations pertinent to Church government under *specified* restrictions, and under no other restrictions. There is not here a delegation of enumerated powers accompanied by a general reservation as in the case of the federal government, but a delegation of general and sweeping powers under enumerated and well-defined restrictions. The whole power to rule and regulate the Church is given to the General conference by the plain terms of the grant, and it is to be held as restricted

---

* Howard's Reports, United States Supreme Court, Vol. XVI, page 308.

only in those particulars in which it was designed not to delegate the power. In what particulars it was designed not to delegate the power must be determined by the terms of the constitution. No limitations can be implied other than those assigned in the instrument itself.

The General conference was at first composed of all the preachers in good standing in the yearly conferences. Afterward membership was restricted to ministers who had been connected with the annual conferences four full calendar years. The General conference was thus constituted up to and including the one held in Baltimore in 1808. No rule or regulation passed by this body was unconstitutional, for the very good reason that there was no constitution, in the sense of that term as now understood and used by our

Church authorities. Its powers to make rules and regulations for the Church were undefined and unlimited. It had "full powers" in all matters pertinent to Church government, and was amenable for its action to no earthly tribunal.

The General conference of 1808 provided that thereafter this supreme council of the Church should be composed of delegates chosen by the annual conferences severally according to a given ratio of representation. The first delegated General conference met in New York in 1812. It was the legitimate successor of the one of 1808, and it succeeded to all the powers of its predecessors, except in so far as those powers were pared down by the limiting terms of the constitution.

To ascertain, therefore, the powers of the General conference in a given case, no search need be made for a specific warrant for the particular rule which it is proposed to enact. It is enough that the constitution does not forbid the rule; for the terms of the grant devolving legislative power upon the General conference are sufficiently comprehensive to authorize the passage of any rule not clearly excepted by the enumerated restrictions.

That this is the scope of the powers delegated to the General conference as they are defined in the terms of the grant, is manifest from sundry considerations, among which may be mentioned:

1. *The grant itself.* Its terms are significant on this point. The General conference "shall have full powers to make rules and regulations for our Church under the following limitations

and restrictions." It may be worth mentioning in this connection that the Constitution of the United States, in delegating to Congress the power to govern the territories, gives authority to "make all needful *rules and regulations;*" and Chief Justice Story, commenting on this clause of the Constitution, says: "The power of Congress over the public territory is clearly exclusive and universal, and their *legislation* is subject to no control."*

According to the very highest authorities, the terms *rules* and *laws* are synonymous, and writers on law as well as lexicographers usually define the one by the other. For example: "Law is a *rule* of action."† "Law is a *rule*, not a transient order."‡ "In its most

* Story on the Constitution, Vol. II, page 189.
† Blackstone's Commentaries, Vol. I, page 38.
‡ Ib., Vol. I, page 44.

extensive sense *law* signifies a *rule* of action. In a more circumscribed sense, as in jurisprudence, it is the *rule* of human actions, that is, of those actions which are the result of the free exercise of intelligence and the will. Law is called a *rule* of action by a metaphor borrowed from mechanics. A rule in its proper sense is an instrument by means of which we draw from one point to another the shortest line possible, which is called a straight line. The rule is used in comparison in the arts to judge whether a line is straight, as it is used in law to judge whether an action is just or unjust. An action is just or right when it conforms to the *rule* which is the *law;* it is unjust when it differs from it, it is not right. And so it is with our will or intention."*

---

* Bouvier's Institutes, Vol. I, page 2.

Says Burlamaqui, a distinguished professor of law in Geneva: "I say that *law is a rule* to signify in the first place what law has in common with counsel, and, secondly, to distinguish law from transient orders given by the supreme power which, not being *permanent rules* of conduct, are not properly laws."* WEBSTER defines *law* to be a *rule*, and *ecclesiastical law* to be "a rule of action prescribed for the government of a Church." He defines *rule* to be "that which is established as a principle, standard, or directory; that by which any thing is to be adjusted or regulated, or to which it is to be conformed; that which is settled by authority or custom for guidance and direction. Thus a statute or law is a *rule* of civil conduct; a canon is a *rule* of ecclesi-

* Natural and Politic Law, page 45.

astical government," etc. Worcester defines *law* to be "a *rule* of action, a decree, statute, or custom publicly established, an enactment of a legislative body, a statute, a body of *rules*, or all the *rules* applicable to a given subject." These authorities—and they might be multiplied indefinitely—show not only that there is nothing in a grant of power "to make *rules*" for the government of a community, incompatible with the enactment, *in pursuance of such a grant*, of the very highest forms of law suited to the circumstances of the governed; but that such a grant does *prima facie* invest the body to whom it is made with the highest legislative functions.

Now, what is the scope of "full pow ers to make *rules* for our Church?" Is it power to make merely prudential arrangements "*about the support of the ministry, missionary contributions, etc.?*"* And when, in the exercise of the "full powers," it shall make *rules* in relation to these or any *other* matters, are they to be such *rules* as *must not be enforced* by any sanctions or penalties, leaving it entirely to the inclination of those for whom the rule was made, whether they will heed its mandate or not? Such a construction perverts the meaning of the grant if its terms are to be interpreted in their generally-received sense. Such ordinances of the General conference would be divested of the attributes of *rules* or *laws*, and would be mere *advice* or *counsels* to the Church. Says Burlamaqui: "All laws have two essential parts; the first is the disposition of the law, which expresseth the

* Christian Advocate and Journal, June 18, 1857.

command or prohibition, the second is the sanction which pronounces the penalty, and it is the penalty that gives it the proper and particular force of law. For were the law-maker contented with merely ordaining or forbidding certain things without adding any kind of menace, this would be no longer a law prescribed by authority, but merely a prudent counsel."* Says Bouvier: "Law is a *rule*, because it is the standard of what the law deems right. It is also called a *rule* to distinguish it from *advice* or *counsel*, which may be given even by an inferior, and the law is a precept which all are bound to obey."† Says Blackstone: "Law is called a *rule* to distinguish it from *advice* or *counsel*, which we are at lib-

---

* Natural and Politic Law, page 74.

† Institutes, Vol. I, page 7.

erty to follow or not as we see proper, and to judge upon the reasonableness or unreasonableness of the thing advised; whereas, obedience to the *law* depends not upon our approbation but upon the *maker's will.* *Counsel* is only matter of persuasion—*law* is matter of injunction; *counsel* acts only upon the willing—*law* upon the unwilling also. Hence, *law* is defined to be a *rule.*"* Now, in all candor, was the delegated General conference invested only with *advisory* powers? Is this the measure of "full powers to make *rules* for our Church?" Power to make "regulations" might, perhaps, be so construed, as that term may mean a mere order prescribed for the transaction of business, but the power to make *rules* can not be so understood, especially when

* Commentaries, Vol. I, page 44.

this latter is taken in connection with the former and as the complement of authority. Mark: the General conference "shall have full powers to make rules *and* regulations for our Church," thus distinguishing that which may be established as a principle or standard of action from a mere order prescribed for the transaction of some business. But let it be observed that, according to the foregoing authorities, a *rule* is a *law* and a *law* is a *rule*, and to be either *law* or *rule*, there must be a *sanction* or *penalty* to be visited upon the disobedient; while ordinances, however solemnly and formally enacted, if they are accompanied with no penalty or menace, are not *rules*, but are mere *advice* or *counsel.* And if such was designed to be the utmost scope of authority for the supreme council of the Church, then the grant should have read: "The General conference shall have *full powers* to give *advice* and *counsels* to our Church under the following limitations and restrictions;" but *such* a grant would not have given authority even to make "'*rules* and regulations' about the support of the ministry, missionary contributions, etc.,"* to say nothing of *rules* relating to other matters.

In what sense had the term "RULES" been used in Church phrase among us prior to 1808, when this grant of powers was made? There is no need of proving, what no one will deny, that in all the *prior* history of the Church it was *the* word employed to express the highest forms of law known to the Methodist Discipline. It is, therefore,

* Christian Advocate and Journal, June 18, 1857.

a fair presumption that it is so employed here, unless there is reason for understanding it in a different sense. Indeed, it is used in this identical sense in the very constitution of which this grant of powers constitutes a part, for the fourth restriction is conservative of "RULES"—*rules*, too, which, by certain parties in the Church, are now claimed as *the* terms of membership, and the *only* terms found in the Discipline.*

2. The *nature of the restrictions* confirms this interpretation of the grant. The powers couched in the granting clause are great enough to have the restrictions carved out of them; they would have embraced every thing covered by the restrictions if the restrictions had not been imposed.

* Christian Advocate and Journal, July 22, 1858.

The logical expression on this subject is—*exceptio probat regulam*—the exception proves the rule; that is, if there is a necessity for the exception, it is a proof that the rule would extend to the excepted cases if the exception did not exist. If the General conference who framed the constitution of the Church understood, when they invested the delegated General conference with full powers to make rules and regulations for our Church, that they endowed that body only with authority to make "merely prudential arrangements for the support of the ministry, missionary contributions, etc.," and not with powers embracing the very items which they excepted from the operation of the grant, then was there no need of exceptions, and they are a farce.

3. The *nature of the proviso author-*

izing the alteration of the restrictions demonstrates the correctness of the foregoing construction of the grant. The restrictions imposed on the use of the powers granted, except the first one, may be altered or abolished by the concurrent action of the annual and General conferences. If they were abolished, then the General conference could do whatever it is now inhibited from doing by these restrictions. But the suspension or destruction of the restrictions can not authorize the General conference to *transcend* the powers couched in the grant, but only to work up to them without restraint. It would then have only "full powers to make rules and regulations for our Church;" but in the exercise of these powers it could legally enact whatever it is forbidden to enact by the restrictions themselves, as well as all other rules which may rightfully originate in any ecclesiastical council whatever.

This construction of the grant must be conceded by every one who consistently holds that the "General Rules" are *the* "terms of membership," and that the General conference is inhibited by the fourth restriction from changing them. For if the power granted did not, in the absence of the subsequent restrictions, give the authority to revoke or change the General Rules, then the fourth restriction is without meaning. But the terms of the grant were ample for such purposes, and the General conference had "full powers" to revoke and change the "General Rules of the United Societies" in pursuance of the grant, and could have done so *ad libitum* but for the restriction.

Is it not, therefore, clear—and the appeal is made to candid men of all parties—is it not *clear* that, so far as the granting clause of the constitution is concerned, the delegated General conference is invested with powers sufficiently ample to authorize that body to enact a statutory rule excluding all slaveholders from the Church as well as to make, revoke, or change Disciplinary terms of membership?

The General conference, before it became a delegated body, had full powers to make an exscinding rule on slavery; and as its powers now are commensurate with its powers then, save as restricted by assigned limitations in the constitution, the General conference is now competent to pass such a rule, unless the restrictions upon its powers forbid it.

Now, no judicial principle is better settled than that the acts of law-making bodies are always to be presumed constitutional till the contrary is shown. If this rule holds in construing the acts of legislative bodies under constitutions delegating only enumerated powers and expressly reserving all others, how much more strongly will it hold when under a constitution delegating "full powers" with only enumerated reservations! It is, therefore, incumbent on him who claims that the General conference has no authority to make a rule excluding all slaveholders from the Church to show that the power to enact such a rule is *excepted out* of the full powers conferred by the terms of the grant.

CHAPTER II.

DOES THE CONSTITUTION FORBID THE GENERAL CONFERENCE TO MAKE A RULE EXCLUDING SLAVEHOLDERS FROM THE CHURCH?

THAT it does so directly and in just so many words no one claims, but that it does the same thing indirectly, nevertheless peremptorily, is maintained by men of high position in the Church.

If the constitution contained another Restrictive Rule in the words following, to wit, *The General conference shall not make a rule excluding all slaveholders from the Church*, then it would be plain that the making of such a rule would be an infraction of the very letter and spirit of the law; and yet there must be some restriction upon the powers of the General conference, as really forbidding this action as would the supposed Restrictive Rule, or that body, in pursuance of the grant of powers made to it in the constitution itself, has full authority to pass a prohibiting rule.

The *fourth* Restrictive Rule is the only one claimed as limiting the power of the General conference over the matter of slaveholding in the Church; and it is not claimed that *this* rule says any thing directly on the subject, but that it does protect simple slaveholding in the Church by virtue of its conservative power over the "General Rules." This restriction forbids the General conference to "revoke or change the General Rules of the United Societies."

It has been alleged that a statutory rule excluding all slaveholders from the Church will violate this Restrictive Rule in two ways—that it will be a *double* assault upon the constitution of the Church:

1. It has been argued that the existing "General Rule" on slavery "authorizes" slaveholding, and that a new rule forbidding what this rule "authorizes" will necessarily conflict with its provisions, and must, therefore, revoke or change the "General Rule" on slavery.*

2. It has been assumed not only that such prohibitory rule will institute a new Disciplinary term of membership, but also that *all* the terms of membership are, and of *necessity must be*, comprised *in* the "General Rules," and

* Daily Western Christian Advocate, May 30, 1856.

that, therefore, such an exscinding rule is prohibited by the fourth Restrictive Rule, unless it be made part and parcel of the "General Rules" in the way prescribed in the constitution.*

These allegations, so far as has yet transpired, are exhaustive of the reasons assigned against the *constitutionality* of a statutory rule excluding slaveholders from the Church. They will be examined in their order.

One of the "Rules" *excepted out* from the control of the General conference by the operation of the fourth restriction, prohibits the *buying and selling of men, women, and children, with an intention to enslave them.* The argument founded on this "General Rule" is substantially this: The "General

*Christian Advocate and Journal, July 22, 1858, *et al.*

Rule," by prohibiting the buying and selling of slaves and not prohibiting the holding of slaves, does, thereby, "authorize" slaveholding, so that a rule forbidding it would contravene the authority here given to hold slaves, and thus revoke or change the General Rule itself—a thing forbidden by the restriction. This argument, which I have aimed to state in its clearest and strongest form, embodies the chief reason assigned at the General conference of 1856 against the constitutionality of a new chapter laying additional embargoes on slavery, as may be seen from the speeches made to defeat the proposed legislation.

The argument may be reduced to the following propositions; namely,

1. The General Rule prohibits slave-*buying* and slave-*selling*.

2. The General Rule does not prohibit *slaveholding.*

3. The General Rule, by prohibiting slave-buying and slave-selling and not prohibiting slaveholding, does, thereby, "authorize" slaveholding; consequently,

4. A rule prohibiting slaveholding will be *incompatible* with the existing General Rule, and in violation of "authority" given by it to hold slaves; and, therefore,

5. The General conference has no power to make a rule prohibiting slaveholding.

The truth of the *first* proposition is generally conceded, though a few are found who claim that the rule was designed to apply only to the case of persons kidnapped in Africa and offered for sale in this country. The truth of the *second* proposition has been denied, though it would seem on insufficient grounds. When the law which is now, for substance, comprised in the General Rule was enacted, it was not understood to be prohibitive of *slaveholding;* for at the same time, and by the same body of men, another rule was enacted which did in plain terms prohibit slaveholding; a work of supererogation, surely, on the hypothesis that this rule did the same thing. Indeed, the whole history of our denominational connection with slavery goes to show that "slave-buying and selling," and slaveholding have always been regarded as proper subjects for separate and distinct rules. They have never been conjoined in the same rule; and while the *existing* General Rule is substantially the same as the law of 1784, the rules relating to slaveholding have undergone repeated and important modifications. These facts, with many others patent in the history of our ecclesiastical legislation, confirm the opinion that the existing General Rule was not designed to prohibit slaveholding.*

The *third* proposition is the hinge on which the whole argument turns. If this be true, the *fourth* follows as a necessary sequence, and these two being established there is no avoiding the conclusion.

---

* The Oregon and California conferences, at their sessions in 1859, both declined to co-operate in any effort to change the General Rule on slavery, and they both *assigned* as the reason for their course that, to their understanding, the General Rule on slavery as it *now* stands *prohibits all sinful slaveholding.*

CHAPTER III.

DOES THE GENERAL RULE AUTHORIZE SLAVEHOLDING?

If the General Rule "authorizes" slaveholding, it does so by a necessary implication, for it contains no words to that direct and obvious intent. But to say that any thing is "authorized" by implication, is to pervert the right use of language. "We *authorize* by a positive and formal declaration to that intent; we *permit* by a direct expression of our will; we *allow* by abstaining to oppose." (Crabb.) Here are clear distinctions in these several terms, which ought not to be ignored. To say that a law which forbids one practice "authorizes" another because it does not forbid that, also, or that it even *permits* it for a like reason, is so to confound the right use of words as to make no distinctions where there are marked differences. A law forbidding a man to steal his neighbor's *horse* does not forbid him to steal his neighbor's *sheep;* yet who will say that the law against horse-stealing "authorizes" sheep-stealing? A law forbidding a man to *steal* does not forbid him to commit a *trespass;* may he, therefore, commit a trespass under authority of law? That the General Rule does not *prohibit* slaveholding, and that it "*authorizes*" slaveholding, are distinct propositions. The one may be true and the other false, which can never be the case where they are equivalent or identical.

The General Rule on slavery declares

not what *shall* be done, but what shall *not* be done. It is, therefore, styled a "negative law." In relation to such laws it was held in the discussions of the last General conference that "*negative laws often authorize infinitely more than they prohibit*,"* and by applying this general principle to the rule on slavery, it was proposed to prove that slaveholding is "authorized" by the paramount law of the Church. In illustration of the doctrine, it was alleged that "*a law prohibiting the circulation of paper money under five dollars prohibits only four denominations, but authorizes the circulation of any numbers beyond even to millions;*" and that "*a law prohibiting the sale of spirituous liquors in less quantities than a quart authorizes the sale of a quart, a*

* Daily Western Christian Advocate, May 30, 1856.

keg, a hogshead, or a thousand hogsheads."*

For the sake of the argument let the correctness of this principle be admitted for a moment. What then? If the foregoing illustrations are pertinent, a "negative law" does not "authorize" any act that differs *in kind* from the act specified in the statute and forbidden by it. For, mark: it is not claimed that the law prohibiting the *circulation* of bills "authorizes" the *manufacturing*, the *banking*, the *counterfeiting*, the *stealing*, nor any other accident or incident of paper money, but simply the "*circulation* of any numbers beyond even to millions." So in relation to the law concerning the sale of spirituous liquors; it "authorizes" the *sale*—nothing more, nothing different.

* Daily Western Christian Advocate, May 30, 1856.

These, then, are "negative laws," not of universal but of partial prohibition, and in this regard are precisely analogous to the "General Rule" on slavery; and it is only claimed for them that they "authorize," in relation to classes of bills and quantities of liquors *not specified* in the law, the *same kind* of action which they prohibit relative to classes of bills and quantities of liquors which *are* specified in the law. When, therefore, a negative law is universal in its terms, it can "authorize" nothing, and when a negative law is one of partial prohibition, whatever it "authorizes" must be restricted to such matters, not covered by the limiting terms of the law, as are the *same in kind* as that prohibited. Now, apply these principles and illustrations to the construction of the General Rule on slavery. This rule does not *utterly* forbid the buying and selling of men, women, and children, but forbids only such cases as are accompanied with an intention to enslave those bought and sold. What, then, does this "negative law" of partial prohibition "authorize" consistently with the foregoing illustrations? SLAVEHOLDING? Nay, verily. If the rule prohibited *slaveholding* under *certain specified circumstances*, then it would be analogous to hold that it "authorizes" slaveholding under all *other* circumstances. But if the existing rule "authorizes any thing in harmony with these illustrations, it is the "*buying* and *selling* of men, women, and children, with an intention to" *free* them. A specific kind of buying and selling is prohibited, and thereby all other kinds of buying and selling are "authorized;" but there is no authority given for *slaveholding*, even admitting the principle of construction to be sound. *This* construction places that which is prohibited and that which is authorized in some sort of correlation, and is precisely analogous to the foregoing construction of the "negative laws" relating to the circulation of bank-bills and to the sale of spirituous liquors.

But the principle of construction is itself unsound. There is a grand fallacy underlying the argument based on these illustrations. A law prohibiting the circulation of bank-bills of a less denomination than five dollars does *not* "authorize" the circulation of bills of any greater denomination. A law prohibiting the sale of spirituous liquors in less quantities than a quart does *not* "authorize" the sale of a quart nor of any greater quantity. The utmost that can be said is this: the law forbidding the circulation of the small bills goes to show that, prior to its enactment, it was not *unlawful* to circulate bills of a less denomination than five dollars. If such a law "authorizes" the circulation of five-dollar bills and all denominations beyond, then a subsequent law forbidding the circulation of these larger denominations, or any one of them, would be incompatible with the pre-existing law, and an infraction of rights granted under it, and, being thus in conflict with the former law, it would necessarily *repeal* it, for a *later* law repeals all *conflicting older* ones. So, also, of the law concerning the sale of spirituous liquors. It does not "authorize" the sale of any quantity, but only *implies* that before it was enacted liquors might lawfully be sold in quantities therein forbidden. The authority to sell liquors in all quantities is a condition *precedent* to a restriction upon its sale, and can not therefore arise from the prohibitory law. Indeed, in these cases and in all similar cases, the right to do what is not forbidden comes not from a prohibitory statute or "negative law," but is necessarily antecedent to it, and is derived either from the natural right of every man to do whatever is not contrary to law, or else from some specific act or grant of legislation to that intent. So far, then, from its being true that "*negative laws authorize infinitely more than they prohibit*," just the converse is true, that they prohibit infinitely more than they "authorize," for they authorize *nothing*, absolutely

NOTHING—and any argument based on such an assumption is utterly worthless.

Moreover, if this doctrine concerning the scope of "negative laws" is correct, it applies to *other* "General Rules," as well as to the one on slavery. Apply this principle of interpretation to the "General Rule" on the observance of the Sabbath. It forbids *the profaning the day of the Lord either by doing ordinary work therein or by buying or selling.* This is a "negative law," of but partial prohibition, and in this respect is precisely analogous to the "General Rule" on slavery. It forbids a member of the Church to do *ordinary work* or to *buy* or *sell* on the Sabbath day. It forbids nothing more, nothing different. Now, are these descriptive terms exhaustive of the catalogue of deeds, which, when done on the Sabbath, are profanations of that holy day? What of hunting, fishing, innocent amusements of every kind, traveling for pleasure, social visiting, etc.? These practices may be indulged innocently enough on other days, but who will say that they well comport with the fourth commandment of the decalogue? But on the principle that partial prohibition gives general *license*, this rule, by prohibiting *ordinary work* and *buying* and *selling*, and prohibiting no *other* violations of the Sabbath, does "authorize" the whole catalogue of profanations of the day of the Lord, which can not be legitimately referred to the one or the other of these classes specified in the rule, and it so fully and clearly "authorizes" them that a rule prohibiting them or any one of them would be in positive conflict with this

"General Rule" itself, and would, therefore, be unconstitutional so long as the existing rule remains unchanged. Who does not see that such an interpretation arrays this organic law of the Church in direct hostility to the divine law written by God's own finger amid the thunderings and lightnings of Sinai? And yet these unprohibited violations of the Sabbath are as clearly and fully "authorized," indeed "authorized" precisely in the same way and to the same extent by this "General Rule" as is slaveholding "authorized" by the "General Rule" on slavery, and any rule of the General conference, or any Disciplinary measures by the executive authorities of the Church interfering with these licensed profanations of the Sabbath would as surely invade *rights* guaranteed to the membership by the paramount law of the Church as would a simple rule of Discipline excluding all slaveholders from her communion.

A rule of interpretation so unsafe in practice must be unsound in theory. Nay, more, *it is vicious.* Better, far better have no prohibitive laws, unless they specify in detail every actual and possible *cognate vice;* for the very moment a prohibition is laid upon *one* of a class, license is given by this very prohibition to practice all the rest, and, thenceforth, however detestable, they may claim the sanction and authority of law. And worse still, no subsequent law forbidding one of these "authorized" sins can be enacted without its very enactment operating a repeal of the "negative law," through whose provisions, or rather *lack* of provisions, these sins were "authorized." Suppose the rule, instead of consisting of a simple prohibition, comprised also an additional clause, specifically licensing the things which it is alleged the prohibitive clause itself "authorizes," would this second clause give the law any additional scope? Most certainly not. The law has the same meaning *without* it as *with* it. The license is in the prohibitive clause; while *that* stands the license must stand. To abolish the license the prohibition must itself be abolished. And to abolish the prohibition would remove the embargo laid upon the vices enumerated in the rule abolished, and thenceforth *they* become "authorized." So absurd a doctrine will be owned by no body when thus nakedly stated; but if this dogma concerning "authority" given by "negative laws" does not imply all this, it requires to be shown how it can be reconciled with any other hypothesis.

Now, if the General Rule on slavery contained an additional clause in these words, "*Nevertheless, members of the Church may hold slaves,*" the meaning of the rule would be identical to that claimed for it *now* on the simple score of its prohibitive clause. So long, therefore, as the law of the Church prohibits the *traffic* in slaves, so long it authorizes *slaveholding*. Admit, then, that "negative laws," by prohibiting one vice, do thereby authorize all kindred vices, and that the General Rule on slavery "authorizes" slaveholding in consequence, and it follows that a law forbidding slaveholding and another law forbidding the slave traffic are incompatible; and, therefore, the passage of a prohibitive rule either *with* or *with-*

out the Restrictive Rule process, will necessarily abrogate the existing rule against buying and selling of men, women, and children, with an intention to enslave them.

But all argument aside, there is one fact which must be conclusive against the assumption that slaveholding is "authorized" by the General Rule on slavery. It is a fact that the law against *slave-buying* and *slave-selling* now comprised in the General Rule; and *another* and distinct law against *slaveholding*, were both enacted by the Christmas conference of 1784. If the law against the slave traffic "authorizes" slaveholding *now* it did the same thing *then*, and the case presents the singular inconsistency of the same body of men at the same time enacting two distinct laws, the one clearly "authorizing" slaveholding and the other as clearly prohibiting it. Did the Christmas conference do so foolish a thing as that? NEVER. The law against the buying and selling did *not* "authorize" slaveholding in 1784, and the existing General Rule, identical in sense and almost so in words, *does not* "authorize" slaveholding in the year of grace 1860.

Is it not, therefore, clear that the General Rule against the traffic does not "authorize" slaveholding? If so, then a new rule prohibiting slaveholding will not be incompatible with its provisions; and, therefore, so far as the General Rule on slavery contains any thing to the contrary, the General conference is competent to enact a simple rule of Discipline which will exclude all slaveholders from the Church.

CHAPTER IV.

GENERAL RULES AND TERMS OF MEMBERSHIP.

A SECOND staple argument against an exscinding statutory rule, produced at the General conference of 1856, and on which a thousand changes have been rung since, relates to the matter of *new terms of membership*.*

It is claimed that a rule excluding slaveholders from the Church will institute a new term or condition of membership, and it is alleged that no *new* term of membership can be established but in the manner prescribed for a

* Daily Western Christian Advocate, May 28 and 30, 1856, and editorials of the Christian Advocate and Journal since 1856.

change of the constitution itself, that is, by a two-thirds vote of the General conference, either preceded or followed by a three-fourths vote of all the members of the several annual conferences who shall be present and vote on the proposition.

The argument when reduced to form stands thus:

1. The General conference is not competent to make a rule of Discipline which will institute a new term of membership in the Church.

2. A rule excluding all slaveholders will institute a new term of membership; therefore,

3. The General conference is not competent to pass such an exscinding rule.

Now, whether the major premiss of this argument is true or false depends entirely on the terms of the constitution itself. The Church through her organic law says substantially to every one seeking admission to her communion: *The General conference has full powers to make rules and regulations for the Church under the limitations and restrictions enumerated in the six Restrictive Rules, and under no other limitations and restrictions. So long as its rules and regulations do no violence to these enumerated restrictions its authority in ecclesiastical affairs is supreme. Are you willing to subject yourself to such a supervision and submit to such a control? On no other terms can you be admitted.* And every man who crosses the threshold of the Church does so, giving satisfactory assurances of his willingness to observe and keep her rules so long as he remains in her fellowship—

her rules not only as they may then exist, but as they may be lawfully modified from time to time thereafter. He then enters her pale, making a solemn covenant with the Church to abide the action of the General conference in the legitimate exercise of its powers to make rules and regulations for the government of his conduct; and whatever rules may be ordained in harmony with the terms of the constitution, and whatever new terms of membership such rules may institute, they are only such conditions of membership as the very nature of the compact between the parties anticipates and provides for; for a condition *precedent* to membership at all, and one of the grounds of his admission to the bosom of the Church, is a stipulation that the General conference should have the right to exercise over him these governmental functions. In the words of the father of Methodism, "*They joined me on these terms; none needs to submit to it unless he will; every preacher and every member may leave me when he pleases, but while he chooses to stay it is on the same terms that he joined me at the first.*"*

Now, if by a rule of Discipline which will institute a new term of membership be meant a rule which contravenes or changes this compact, virtually entered into by and between the Church and each individual member on his entering her communion, then the first proposition or major premiss of the argument is unquestionably true. But taking the phrase in this sense it becomes necessary, in maintaining the

* Wesley's Works, Vol. V, page 221.

truth of the second proposition, or minor premiss, to show that the General conference is forbidden, by the restrictions on its powers, to make a rule prohibiting slaveholding; for if the General conference is not thus inhibited, then the enacting and enforcing of such a rule will be no violation of the covenant between the parties, and can not, therefore, in that sense institute a new term of membership.

But the phrase "term of membership" may mean a *condition*, by the *observance* of which a member so far forth has a *right* to remain in the Church, or by the *non*-observance of which he forfeits such right. This is the sense in which it is generally employed, and in which it will be used henceforth in this argument. In this sense a rule may be said to institute a *new* term of membership for the communicant, when it enjoins *new* duties or entails *new* liabilities—duties which members were not required to perform, and liabilities to which they were not subject when he joined the Church. And it is difficult to conceive of any rule of Discipline either enlarging or restricting the rights and privileges of members, or in any way modifying their duties and liabilities, which would not in this sense institute a *new* term or condition of membership. If members do not voluntarily leave the Church they must remain in it on conditions and under circumstances differing from those existing before the rule was ordained. To whatever subject the rule may relate, and to whatever extent it may apply, and whether it be the rule in its original form or as modified by subsequent legislation, and however trivial, comparatively, may be the matter enjoined or forbidden by it, still if the rule be of any *binding* force whatever, and the Discipline be faithfully administered, the *ultimatum* in every case is either *obedience* to the rule or *exclusion* from the Church. Does not every rule, therefore, which relates to the conduct of members and is of *binding force* make a term of membership? Does not every such *new* rule make a *new* term of membership? Now, if every such *new* rule makes a *new* term of membership, and no new term of membership can be instituted in the Discipline by the General conference, then the grant of power given by the constitution to this delegated body to make "rules" for the Church, is the *merest pretension.*

Taking the phrase "new terms of membership" in this latter sense, then the truth of the *second* proposition or *minor* premiss of the argument is admitted; though a very large and intelligent portion of the antislavery men of the Church deny it, alleging that the Discipline as it is, *properly administered*, would exclude all slaveholders from the Church. There certainly is not now any *specific* rule of Discipline forbidding members of the Church to hold slaves, and any rule passed now disqualifying a slaveholder for Church fellowship simply for the reason that he *is* a slaveholder would institute a condition of membership not *clearly* and *explicitly* in the Discipline.

In this view, however, in order to maintain the truth of the *first* proposition, it requires to be shown that *every* rule which in this latter sense will inaugurate a new term of membership must be made by the Restrictive Rule process. It is not enough to show that the rule makes that a condition of membership which was not so before; but it must be shown that the power to make the given rule was *excepted out* of the "full powers" conveyed in the terms of the grant.

This argument against the constitutionality of an exscinding statutory rule is very clearly and forcibly put by the distinguished editor of the *Advocate and Journal*. He says:

"The whole logic of this subject is in a 'nut-shell,' and all the fumbling of partisan sophistry can not make it obscure to the good sense of the Church; the General Rules are your terms of membership, and your only terms—they say so themselves; your Restrictive Rules say you can not change them but by a given process prescribed by the Restrictive Rules; these General Rules contain but one law or condition of membership which has respect to slavery—it prohibits the slave traffic but not slaveholding; to introduce the latter prohibition is to make a new General Rule or condition of membership never known among us since the organization of the Church; it must, therefore, be done by the process of the Restrictive Rules if done at all. . . The man who contends that a new term of membership can be enacted without the Restrictive Rule process, provided the new term is smuggled into some other part of the Discipline than the General Rules, where it belongs—the best we can say of him is that he is not to be reasoned with."*

This logic is invincible if the premises are well taken. The validity of the whole argument, however, depends on a proposition, the truth of which is assumed when it ought to have been proved. The point vital to the case,

*Christian Advocate and Journal, July 22, 1858.

and which the writer has taken for granted, is this, namely: "General Rules" and "terms of membership" are equivalent and convertible terms, from which it is concluded that the fourth Restrictive Rule, which forbids the General conference to "*revoke or change the General Rules of the United Societies*," means *now* just what it would mean if it forbade the General conference to "*revoke or change the terms of membership in the Methodist Episcopal Church.*"

This doctrine, so far as appears, is *new*. It does not seem to have been held to any important extent, if, indeed, it obtained at all, till within a period very recent in the history of Methodism, while, on the other hand, from the organization of the Church onward we are confronted at almost every step with "things hard to be understood" on any such hypothesis. In saying this there is no impeachment of the testimony of the venerable and venerated worthies whose statements, gathered in 1858, have been given to the world as conclusive of its antiquity.* They testify truthfully to their own understanding of the matter, and, doubtless, a list of twice the number, composed of ministers of equal age, talents, and character, could very easily be obtained in the same manner whose testimony would support just the opposite view. But whether the doctrine be old or new is of very little moment. It is not true because it is old nor false because it is new; these qualities are intrinsic and not accidents of time.

* Appeal to the Methodist Episcopal Church on Slavery, pages 16, 17, 18.

Moreover, this doctrine is, in the estimation of some, a very *dangerous* one, fraught with untold disaster to the Church. But disastrous consequences which different parties may conceive as liable to follow the prevalence of this or that interpretation of the constitution of the Church do not determine the import of the instrument itself. The doctrine is not only new and dangerous, but it is *erroneous*, supported by neither pertinent facts nor sound reasoning, but contradicted by them both.

Before proceeding to consider the scope and authority of the fourth restriction, it may be proper to recur to the subject treated in the first chapter for the purpose of answering the most *plausible* objection yet made to the view there taken. The objection is considered in this place rather than in the chapter on that particular subject, because of its intimate relation to the fourth restriction, and to the question of "terms of membership."

With a view to set aside the doctrines maintained in the first chapter and to prove that the General conference of 1808 did not understand the terms of the grant, even in the absence of restrictions, as investing the delegated General conference with any other than power to make merely prudential provisions for the administration of rules prescribed in the organic law of the Church, an astute writer in the *Pittsburg Advocate*, whose articles are quoted in the main in the "APPEAL," and indorsed by its author as the most logical yet written on the subject, says:

"An attempt was made, however, to

clothe the General conference with the law-making power. The proposition granting power to the delegated General conference, when first presented to that of 1808, read: 'The General conference shall have full powers to make rules, regulations, and *canons* for our Church under the following limitations and restrictions.' Had this proposition been adopted, 'canon' being the proper term to designate a law enacted by ecclesiastical authority, it would have clothed the delegated General conference with the law-making power. But the General conference of 1808, true to its purpose, *refused to adopt the proposition in this form,* and did not adopt it till the term 'canons' was stricken out. By striking out this term, or causing it to be stricken out, it clearly refused to invest the delegated General conference with the law-making power. Its legislative powers are, therefore, merely prudential.

"The General conference of 1808, refusing to clothe the delegated General conference with the law-making power, reserved it to the great body of the ministry, and in the proviso to the Restrictive Rules pointed out the manner in which it should thereafter be exercised. This power, as far as it existed in the Church, had always been in the ministry. With this body it still remains. And no new term of membership can be constitutionally enacted without the concurrent recommendation of three-fourths of all the members of the several annual conferences who shall be present and vote on such recommendation, preceded or followed by a majority of two-thirds of the General conference."*

It is true, as here stated, that the term "canons" was contained in the grant of powers in the constitution, as it was reported by the committee of fourteen to the General conference of 1808, and that it was *struck out* before the constitution was adopted. It is *also* true, though it is not stated by this writer nor by the author of the "Appeal," that the *restrictions* upon the powers

*Appeal to the Methodist Episcopal Church on Slavery, page 13.

which it was proposed to grant were the *same* in the constitution when "first presented" to the General conference of 1808 as they are in the *existing* constitution, with the exception of the *first*, and that was modified so as to *enlarge* rather than diminish the powers of the delegated General conference; and *especially* was the *fourth* restriction contained in it in *precisely the same words* as at present.*

The foregoing quotation states three things worthy of notice: 1. That a deliberate *attempt* was made to invest the General conference with the *law-making* power by authorizing it to make "canons" for our Church. 2. That by striking the term "canons" from the grant such power was *clearly refused* to the General conference, and *reserved*

* Journal of General Conference for 1808, page 82.

to the great body of the ministry; and, 3. That the *retention* of this term would have invested the General conference with the *law-making* power—with power to enact new terms of membership, etc.

Now, if the scope of the fourth restriction was understood *then* to be any thing like that claimed for it *now*, it is passing strange that a committee of fourteen, consisting of such men as EZEKIEL COOPER, JOHN WILSON, GEORGE PICKERING, JOSHUA SOULE, WILLIAM M'KENDREE, WILLIAM BURKE, WILLIAM PHOEBUS, JOSIAS RANDALL, PHILIP BRUCE, JESSE LEE, STEPHEN G. ROSZEL, NELSON REED, JOHN M'CLASKEY, and THOMAS WARE,* would insert it in a constitution which they had drawn with deliberate design to invest the General conference with the

* Journal of General Conference of 1808, page 79.

"law-making power"—with power to make, revoke, and change the terms of membership in the Church. By every principle of legal interpretation the fourth Restrictive Rule means *now* just what it meant in 1808. No lapse of time can change its import. Its meaning in 1808 was just what its authors understood it to mean. If this restriction forbids the General conference to make rules instituting new disciplinary terms of membership, it does so because those who made the rule *designed* it thus to restrict the powers of that body. But it is past belief that a committee of intelligent men in attempting "to clothe the General conference with the law-making power," and, therefore, with power to make rules instituting new terms of membership, and who had deliberately framed the granting clause of the con stitution with that intent, should propose in the same instrument a Restrictive Rule framed with equal deliberation, and *designed* by its authors to absolutely inhibit the delegated General conference from exercising the identical power with which they were laboring to invest it. Indeed, if it be true, as is here alleged, that they sought to invest the General conference with such authority and yet proposed this restriction upon the powers granted, they either *stultified* themselves or else to their comprehension this provision had nothing of the scope claimed for it now, and did not interfere at all with the exercise of the powers they wished to delegate. And, on this hypothesis, the General conference must have entertained views concerning the restriction in entire harmony with those of the committee; for it is asserted that "*by striking out*" *the term* "*canons*" they "*clearly refused to invest the General conference with the law-making power;*" whereas, if the prohibition to "revoke or change the General Rules of the United Societies," which was proposed as a part of the constitution, absolutely inhibited any rule affecting the terms of membership in the Church, ten thousand "canons" would have been innocent of mischief, for this sweeping restriction would have "*spiked*" them all; or, in other words, if the action of the General conference of 1808 in striking the term "canons" from the grant, as reported by the committee, is rightly interpreted by this writer and his indorser, then the *history* of the case is absolutely demonstrative against their construction of the fourth Restrictive Rule; for it was by striking out this term and not by imposing the fourth restriction that the power to make rules instituting new terms of membership was *withheld* from the delegated General conference, and *reserved* to the great body of the ministry.

But is there no mistake in saying that the term "canons" was struck out for the purpose of thwarting the attempt to invest the delegated General conference with legislative powers? Was it done with such design? Was any change made in the scope of delegated powers by expunging it from the grant? What is the signification of "canon?" Etymologically it means a *rule.* "The sense of *canon* is that which is set or established. 1. In *ecclesiastical affairs* a law or *rule* of doctrine or discipline enacted by a council and confirmed by the sovereign; a decision of matters in religion, or a regulation of policy or discipline, by a general or provincial council. 2. A law or *rule* in general." (WEBSTER.) A *canon* is, therefore, a Church *rule*—a rule enacted by ecclesiastical authority, nothing more; and "the proposition granting power to the delegated General conference when first presented to that of 1808" would have read, when translated into plain English, "The General conference shall have full powers to make rules, regulations, and *rules* for our Church under the following limitations and restrictions." "Rules" and "canons"—the one English, the other Greek—are synonymous; to have retained both, would have made the expression tautological, conveying no meaning that it would not have conveyed with either word, no matter which, expunged; and as the Methodist Discipline was to be in English rather than in Greek, "canons" was struck out and "rules" retained. There was another change precisely analogous to this, made in the granting clause; for the *record* shows that, according to the report of the committee, the powers were to be used under *limitations* and restrictions; but, by the same record, it appears that the General conference refused to adopt it till the term "limitations" was struck out.* Will any one claim that this term was expunged to *enlarge* the powers of the conference by permitting the exercise of its functions *without* "limitations?" The claim is

* Journal of General Conference for 1808, page 82 and page 89.

just as valid in the one case as in the other, and it is good for nothing in either, as the sole object in both cases was, doubtless, to dispose of redundant terms.

It is conceded by the writers quoted above that if the term "canons" had been *retained* the grant would clearly have invested the General conference with power to make new terms of membership, and that too notwithstanding the fourth restriction. But whatever powers would have been given by authorizing the General conference to make rules, regulations, and *canons* for our Church, *are* given by the grant as it now stands; and if the grant, as *first presented* to the General conference of 1808, "would have clothed the delegated General conference with the law-making power," as is alleged in the foregoing extract from the "APPEAL," it is a logical sequence from which there is no escape that the grant *now* endows that body with this identical power. So that in whatever light this opposing argument be viewed, it makes nothing against the construction of the constitution claimed in this little book. For by claiming that the General conference of 1808, in being "true to its purpose," found it necessary to strike the term "canons" from the grant so as to deny to the *delegated* General conference the power to make new terms of membership, it is virtually conceded that the fourth Restrictive Rule was not *designed* for that purpose; and also by claiming that the retention of the term "canons" would have invested the delegated General conference with such powers, it is virtually conceded that the fourth Restrictive Rule does not *forbid* the making of new terms of membership, else that restriction would have neutralized all possible power to that effect conveyed by authority to make "canons," and the retention of this term would not have clothed the General conference with any law-making power. And this is not all, but by admitting that the grant of power to make rules, regulations, and *canons* for our Church would have clothed the delegated General conference with power to make new terms of membership, it is virtually conceded that the delegated General conference has the same measure of legislative power *now;* for there is ample authority for saying that *expunging* the term "canons" from the grant did not in the least modify the scope of the powers delegated. So much for the "*history* of the Restrictive Rule," claimed as "proof point blank"* that the General conference has no power to enact new terms of membership.

But to return to the argument introduced to prove that the fourth restriction inhibits all change of the terms of membership by the General conference: is it true that "General Rules" and "terms of membership" are equivalent and convertible phrases? May the latter be substituted for the former in the fourth restriction and leave its meaning and scope unchanged? If so, the argument is good; if not, then it is good for nothing.

Disciplinary rules may all be referred to two classes: 1. Those relating to

---

* Appeal to the Methodist Episcopal Church on Slavery, page 12.

the *moral* conduct of members *as Christians;* and, 2. Those relating to the *order* and *discipline peculiar* to the Methodist Episcopal Church. To the former belong the "General Rules;" not called *general* in the sense of comprehending *all* the rules in the Discipline of general application and obligation, but a specific and limited set of rules drawn up by Mr. Wesley for his societies composed of members of the Church of England, and which rules were by *him* denominated, "The General Rules of the United Societies." In these rules Christian duties, *as taught in the Scriptures*, are set forth in generic and sweeping principles. They constitute perhaps the best epitome of the laws of the Christian life ever written by an uninspired man; but they are *only* an epitome, by no means measuring up to the fullness and particularity of the Divine word, either in their prohibitions or injunctions, leaving a great variety of duties to be enforced by specific rules to that intent. That this is their entire scope as used in the constitution of the Church is quite plain from the fact that the General conference of 1808, in adopting the fourth restriction, put the phrase "General Rules of the United Societies" in quotation marks,* thus indicating that it was to be taken in a *limited* and *technical* sense. Rules other than those comprised in this special code are not within the purview of the fourth restriction, and may, therefore, be revoked or changed by the General conference.

If, indeed, it be conceded that the

* Journal of General Conference for 1808, page 89.

"General Rules," when they forbid "evil of every kind," authorize administrative rules to apply and enforce this prohibition in its broadest sense, and that its scope is not restricted to the particular forms of evil enumerated under it; and if it be conceded that, when they command "doing good of every possible sort," they authorize administrative rules applying this injunction to whatever in the judgment of the General conference comes legitimately under that head, whether it be detailed in the specifications under it or not, then are the provisions of the "General Rules" sufficiently comprehensive to cover all needful terms of membership relating to moral and Christian conduct; though even then they would furnish no authority for rules and regulations purely denominational. But such a construction will not be conceded by those who contend that slavery can be outlawed in the Church only by the Restrictive Rule process. They claim a construction which limits the evil of *every kind* to just such matters of conduct as are specified under it, and by so doing they have estopped themselves from any such liberal construction as will justify a specific rule to prohibit any evil or to enforce any duty not distinctly named in the "General Rules."

Now, if I do not misread and misjudge both law and history, the "General Rules of the United Societies" do not *now* comprise all the terms of membership contained in the Discipline, neither *did* they at any one period in the history of American Methodism, either before or since the organization of a General conference with delegated

powers. And this is equally true whether we consider the case of one proposing either to join the Church on trial or to be received in full connection, or as having already attained to membership in the Church, as is apparent from the following illustrations:

1. The "General Rules" do not require persons wishing to be admitted on trial, to be well recommended by one the preacher knows; or else to have met twice or thrice in class; and yet the preacher is forbidden by a statutory rule of the Church to receive him on trial unless he have one or the other of these requisites.

2. The "General Rules" do not require a candidate for membership to come recommended by a leader with whom he has met at least six months on trial; nor do they require that he

should have been on trial at all. Moreover, they do not require him to give satisfactory assurances of the correctness of his faith and of his willingness to observe and keep the rules of the Church. Dr. Emory, in his History of the Methodist Discipline, speaking of changes made in 1840, says this "was *added* to the *requisites* for admission into the Church."* Neither do the General Rules make baptism a condition precedent to membership. Dr. Emory, mentioning changes of the Discipline made in 1836, says: "It was *now* made a *requisite* to membership that candidates 'have been baptized.'"† And what is more, the General Rules not only do not make baptism a condition *precedent* to membership as does the

* History of the Discipline, last edition, page 198.
† History of the Discipline, last edition, page 198.

statute law of the Church, but they do not enjoin baptism at all, nor do they even recognize the existence of such an ordinance. The "APPEAL" claims that as they enjoin attendance upon "*all the ordinances of God,*" they, therefore, require baptism,* and authorize the General conference to enforce its observance by specific statute, notwithstanding it is omitted from the list of ordinances embraced in the rules themselves. But no one ought to claim this interpretation unless he will admit, also, that, by forbidding evil of *every kind*, they authorize the General conference by specific enactment to apply this sweeping prohibition to *other* evils than those enumerated under it. Baptism is very properly a condition *precedent*

* Appeal to the Methodist Episcopal Church on Slavery, page 15.

to membership, and having been once observed is not to be repeated. But the "General Rule" concerning ordinances was made for persons who, having *gained* admission to the Church, desire to *continue* therein; and the rule requires them to *continue* to evidence their desire of salvation by *attending* upon divine ordinances. The whole tenor of the requirement shows that the evidence to meet the demand must be a *continuing* evidence; and this would strictly require a repetitious observance of baptism, no less than of the other ordinances—a requirement incompatible with the nature and obligations of Christian baptism. There can, therefore, be no reasonable doubt that baptism was omitted by design from the catalogue of ordinances enjoined by the "General Rules."

Here, then, are *two* alternate conditions of admission on trial, and some *half dozen* more of admission to full membership, no one of which is found in any provision of the "General Rules;" and still they are all and singular made indispensable prerequisites to Church membership by rules which do not come within the purview of the fourth restriction, and which the General conference may, therefore, revoke or change at pleasure.

3. In relation to members of the Church it may be observed:

(1.) There are special acts or matters of conduct made terms of membership by statutory rules of the Church which are not so set forth in the "General Rules;" as, for instance: *a.* Inveighing against the doctrines and discipline of the Church; *b.* Refusing to submit disputed accounts to arbitration; *c.* Refusing to abide the award of arbiters on disputed accounts; *d.* Refusing to await the time fixed by a committee for the payment of an adjusted account; *e.* Refusing to give such additional security for the payment of an adjusted account as a committee may determine. It is not intimated that these conditions are improper or unscriptural; nay, they are highly proper, especially as the Church forbids her members to go "to law" for the settlement of financial disputes; but they are certainly not named among the evils to be avoided by persons desiring to remain in the communion of the Church.

(2.) In the trial of both ministers and members charged with crime the inquest is not whether the crime is forbidden in the "General Rules," but is it forbidden *in the word of God* as an unchristian practice; herein ignoring the "General Rules," and setting up instead thereof the law of Gód as the measure of morality. And by just so many as the unchristian practices forbidden in the word of God exceed in number those specified and forbidden in the "General Rules," by just so many does this statutory rule institute Disciplinary terms of membership not prescribed in the "General Rules." This rule is based upon a broad principle which should be recognized in the jurisprudence of all Christian Churches, and which is specially set forth by the Wesleyans of England in their Minutes for 1835. It seems that the import and meaning of their rule for the exclusion of members from the society had been made a subject of much controversy during the agitations of the Connection in the years 1834 and 1835, and the conference in the latter year issued a declaration and passed resolutions relating thereto which now constitute their entire law for the expulsion of accused members. The eighth article of this declaration says:

"In the preceding articles of this document reference has been repeatedly made to the *law of God contained in the holy Scriptures,* as furnishing, in the trial of members, that *primary* standard of judgment, by which the innocence or culpability of any particular facts adduced in evidence is ever to be determined. This principle, though obvious and scarcely needing argumentative defense, the conference have advisedly made prominent in this statement of their views. Any conduct in a man professing godliness, which can be shown to be decidedly *condemned by the precepts and principles* of the New Testament, is surely sufficient to justify, if persisted in, the application of a suitable ecclesiastical censure or other penalty to such an individual, *even though it may not have been previously found necessary to make a distinct and specific rule of our own society on that exact mode and form of delinquency*. The New Testament *law of purity*, in reference both to pastors and members of the Christian Church, and with respect both to doctrine and practice, its often-repeated *law of peace*, and *godly quietness*, and its *laws of courtesy*, *brotherly kindness*, and mutual *charity*, as well as its direction that 'all things' should 'be done decently and in order,' and its requirement of reasonable submission on the part of Church members to the Scriptural 'rule' of those who are 'over them in the Lord;' these are *standing enactments* of the Gospel, binding on all Christian communities, and therefore binding on the Methodist societies without exception. Any obstinate violation of them must be suitably visited when proved, or else the authority of Christ himself, as the Lord and master of our department of his spiritual house, will be criminally set at naught, and he will have just cause to say to the ministers and pastors of our community, as he did to one of old time, 'I have somewhat against thee.'"*

And should any course of conduct condemned by the precepts and principles of the *holy Scriptures* obtain in the Methodist Episcopal Church, through a failure of the administrator of discipline to apply these precepts and principles to its extirpation, then the General conference, as the guardian of the purity and honor of the Church, not only has the *right* but it becomes her most imperative and solemn *duty* to provide by a specific rule for that exact mode and form of delinquency.

(3.) Another rule, though no longer in the Discipline, is highly illustrative

---

*Grindrod's Compendium of the Laws and Regulations of Wesleyan Methodism, pages 150, 151.

of the fact that "General Rules" and "terms of membership" are not identical, and that the General conference has deemed itself competent to revoke and change the latter, though forbidden to revoke or change the former. The rule alluded to is the one which prohibited members of the Church from marrying irreligious persons. A forfeiture of membership was the penal sanction of this rule, and several instances of the exclusion of otherwise worthy members of the Church for its breach have fallen under my own observation, and that, too, in cases where the Discipline was administered by the "fathers." This rule was in force from the organization of the Church till 1836, when it was "revoked" by the General conference "*without the Restrictive Rule process.*" It constituted a term of membership both before and after the adoption of the "constitution," yet, not being a "General Rule," the General conference was guilty of no contempt of the fourth restriction in *revoking* it.

(4.) Conformity to the *order* of Discipline is obligatory upon members of the Church, and disobedience thereto, if persisted in, works a forfeiture of Church membership in pursuance of a *statutory* law of the Discipline. Certain police regulations for the harmonious movement of the various departments of the Church are indispensable to her power and perpetuity. The General conference has, by the constitution of the Church, exclusive authority to prescribe these regulations, and, as a sequence, to enforce obedience thereto by appropriate penalties. To illustrate: suppose a private member of the Church, believing himself called to preach, should disregard the *order* of the Church, and commence preaching and administering the sacraments without being duly authorized thereto in the manner pointed out in the Discipline, and should persist therein, he violates no "General Rule," and yet the statute law provides for his exclusion for disobedience to the *order* of the Church.* In fact, no rules of Church *order* are prescribed in the "General Rules," and what is more, no

* Since the above was written, Bishop Morris has published an admirable little book on "*Church Polity*," on the 33d page of which he says: "*Any member who . . . persists in disobedience to the order of Discipline, renders himself liable to reproof,* 1, *by his leader,* 2, *by his pastor; then, if not reclaimed, he should be cited to answer before the society or a select number, and if found guilty and incorrigible, the rule is to exclude him.*" A case involving this same principle was before the Genesee conference at its late session. The following question of law was proposed to the President, Bishop Simpson; namely,

such rules can, with any degree of propriety, be inserted in that code. The "General Rules" enforce *moral* duties obligatory on *all* Christians, and, therefore, on *Methodist* Christians, and *such* rules may without impropriety be inserted among them; but they recognize no form of Church government, and no peculiarities of Church organization; neither *can* they without putting off their distinguishing characteristics, as will be shown more fully hereafter.

"*Can members of our Church go by themselves in any numbers and organize for the purpose of holding public religious meetings independent of our Church and its authorities?*" To this both Bishop Simpson and Bishop Morris answered, No. And Bishop Morris goes on to say that in such cases "*the regular way is, 1, to reprove them, and then, unless they repent, 2, to cite them individually to trial before a committee for disobedience to the order of Discipline.*" And in this opinion Bishop Simpson concurred. (See proceedings of Genesee conference in Northern Advocate, October 12, 1859.

Now, as rules of order are necessary not only to the efficiency, but to the very existence of the Church, and as such rules are not and *can* not be prescribed in the "General Rules," it follows that there always have been, are now, and, of necessity, always will be terms of membership outside of the "General Rules," and which depend solely for their origin, nature, and perpetuity upon the action of the General conference; for the constitution makes no provision for the concurrent action of the annual conferences in relation to such matters. It provides for such concurrent action on propositions to "revoke or change the *General Rules of the United Societies;*" but from these "Rules" this whole class of conditions of membership is necessarily excluded.

(5.) The rule making attendance at class a condition of membership, highly important and useful as it has been, and indispensable as it still is, to the welfare of the Church, is not one of the "General Rules," and the General conference has no power to make it a "General Rule." The section of the Discipline containing the "General Rules" treats of three separate things: 1. The *nature;* 2. The *design;* 3. The *General Rules* of the United Societies. The "General Rules" are set forth under three principal heads or classes; namely, 1. *Doing no harm, avoiding evil of every kind,* etc.; 2. *Doing good of every possible sort,* etc.; and, 3. *Attending on Divine ordinances.* That the rules named under these three heads constitute what are distinctively called the "General Rules" to the exclusion of all other parts of the section, is plain from two declarations found in the closing paragraph of the section itself. After declaring these to be the General Rules of our societies, then their *distinguishing* characteristics are thus set forth; namely, 1. "*All which we are taught of God to observe even in his written word;*" and, 2. "*All these we know his Spirit writes on truly-awakened hearts.*" Now it is agreed that "*John Wesley always said what he meant;*"* but did Mr. Wesley—does the Methodist Church to-day mean to say that we are *taught of God even in his written word* to observe the details in this section of the Discipline which relate to the organization of classes, the duties of class-leaders, the

*Appeal to the Methodist Episcopal Church on Slavery, page 42, note.

constitution and functions of leaders' meetings, etc.? Or that the Spirit of God *writes all these on truly-awakened hearts?* If *so*, and the doctrine be *true*, then no man can be a Christian and not observe them; if *not*, then they constitute no part of the "General Rules," for *all these* are thus distinguished. And that the *Church* does not understand the rule on class meetings as a mere administrative measure to enforce a requirement of the "General Rules" is plain from this: If the "General Rules" are such as we are taught of God, even in his written word, to observe, as is solemnly affirmed by him who wrote them, then he who violates any one of them contravenes a Divine precept, and is guilty of immoral conduct; but to "willfully and repeatedly neglect to meet in class" is *not* immoral conduct in the judgment of the Church; for when one is laid aside for such neglect, it is specially enjoined on the preacher to show that he is "*excluded for a breach of our rules and not for immoral conduct.*" Again, if the duty of meeting in class is taught in the written word of God, as it must be according to Mr. Wesley, if it be enjoined by the "General Rules," then is class meeting an "*instituted*" means of grace and obligatory upon all Christians; but, according to Mr. Wesley and the Methodist Discipline, it is not an instituted but a "*prudential*" means of grace; not obligatory upon us as *Christians* but as *Methodists.* A man may doubtless be a very good Christian without meeting in class; but he can not be a good Methodist and pursue the same course.

Now, the "General Rules," enjoined as they all are by the written word of God, and written as they all are upon truly-awakened hearts, may be called, after the analogy of the Discipline, "*instituted*" requirements, and are binding upon all Christians alike without regard to their peculiar denominational relations; while other matters in the same section of the Discipline, consisting chiefly of historical statements relating to the origin and design of the United Societies, and the nature of their organization, are of a strictly *prudential* character; are limited and sectarian in their scope; are *not* enjoined in the written word of God; are *not* written on all truly-awakened hearts, and do not, therefore, constitute any portion of the "General Rules of the United Societies."

It has been claimed that the "General Rules" "expressly provide for attendance at class as a condition of membership,"* and for the reason, it is alleged, that by making it "*the duty of the leader to see each person in his class once a week,*" they thereby enjoin "*the correlative duty of every member to be present that he may be seen there.*"† This view assumes that the clause of the Discipline stating it to be the duty of the leader "to *see* each person in his class once a week" is one of the "General Rules"—an assumption more easily made than proved.‡ But for the sake of the argument let

* Christian Advocate and Journal, August 11, 1859, editorial notes appended to Dr. True's article.

† Christian Advocate and Journal, August 4, 1859, editorial notes appended to Moses Hill's article.

‡ Dr. Bond says: "Class meetings as a term of membership and love-feasts may also be abolished

what is *assumed* be conceded, and is the case then made out? Did Mr. Wesley so understand the rule when he framed it? It is a historical fact, according to the authority of both Bishop Coke and Bishop Asbury, that "at the beginning of Methodism the leader *called* weekly upon each member of his class, in which case twelve were quite sufficient for their inspection."* Afterward, according to the same authority, it was "found abundantly preferable for the whole class to meet the leader *together*, not only for the sake of the leader, but for the good of the people, who by that means

---

without violating any express prohibition in the constitution; for, though the General conference is prohibited from altering the 'General Rules' or our Articles of Religion, neither *class meetings* nor love-feasts *are enjoined by either the one or the other*." (Christian Advocate and Journal, February 4, 1846.)

* History of the Discipline, last edition, page 380.

enjoy the unspeakable advantage of Christian fellowship."* Now, this historical fact shows that in its *origin* the prescribed duty of the leader did *not* involve "the correlative duty of the member to *meet* in class that he might be seen *there*." How comes it to mean that *now?* Are not the words *identical?* When was their meaning changed, and by what authority? So that even admitting, that what is said of classes and of the duties of leaders constitutes a part of the "General Rules," it can not, then, be maintained that they make weekly attendance at class a condition of membership even by *implication*, much less by express declaration.

It is, however, objected to this *whole array*, that in all these cases there are

* History of the Discipline, last edition, page 380.

no terms of membership which are not authorized by the "General Rules," and, that these are merely *administrative* measures. Administrative of what? *Of Bible morality and of the elements of denominational success?* If so, it is granted. This is the legitimate sphere of all ecclesiastical legislation. But if administrative of the specifications of the "General Rules" only, let it be shown what "General Rule" is to be enforced by each of the several administrative rules; and let the whole list be exhausted; for should there be but a single case of different character, it would stand in contradiction of the declaration that "the General Rules are your terms of membership, and your only terms."

The author of the "APPEAL" makes one sweeping answer to the foregoing argument relating to new terms of membership, to which I will give only a passing notice. After denying that the instances produced are *real* cases of the kind, he says: "*If any real ones could be found, they would only prove that the General conference has erred in some instances.*"* Such an argument is not to be refuted. It must go for what it is worth. It may not be amiss to say, however, that it is quite probable that when the General conference enacts a given rule, its action is in pursuance of a deliberate judgment that it has the *right* so to do, and if there are any cases of terms of membership outside the "General Rules," it is proof that in the judgment of that body those "Rules" were

*Appeal to the Methodist Episcopal Church on Slavery, page 15.

not the only terms of membership which might be *lawfully* in the Discipline; and the combined wisdom of that grave and reverend body of men thus tacitly passing its opinion as to the constitutionality of its acts, is of more authority in determining questions of law than the opinion of any one man were he as wise as Solomon.

Most of these rules constituting terms of membership outside of the "General Rules" were made while the General conference had unlimited powers. But this fact strengthens the foregoing argument. For, having *unlimited* powers, it is not likely that much pains would be taken to adapt the rules made to the mere administration of *other* rules in the Discipline, and which other rules they had full powers to revoke or change at pleasure. And if these conditions of membership were in the Discipline, and were allowed to remain outside of the "General Rules," when the restrictions were adopted, it is good proof that the General conference of 1808 did not understand "General Rules" and "terms of membership" to be equivalent and convertible phrases, nor that by adopting the fourth restriction that they put it beyond the power of any delegated General conference to make a rule either establishing, revoking, or changing a Disciplinary term of membership in the Church. These statutory rules are and always have been under the control of the General conference. That body can modify or revoke them at pleasure. If it can revoke, it can restore; if it can change, it can change again; and as a changed rule is in form and in fact a new one, a power to change is a power to originate.

Is it true, then, that the General conference can make no rule or regulation creating a Disciplinary term of membership, and that when such a rule exists outside of the "General Rules" it is "smuggled"* into a place where it does not belong? If so, then the General conference can make no rule or regulation with *binding force.* It can not forbid by specific statute adultery, polygamy, prostitution, or any other sin not named in the "General Rules," and no preacher has any right to expel a member for these crimes on such principles of construction. If any one thinks it can be done let him show by what rule or authority. Besides, such a construction makes the

* Christian Advocate and Journal, July 22, 1858.

General conference of 1808 stultify itself: 1. By giving to a delegated General conference power to legislate, in one rule, and taking it away in another. 2. By exalting the "General Rules" into *sole* conditions of membership and then leaving other terms of membership in the statutes of the Discipline. 3. By giving to preachers in charge more power than it gave to the General conference; for they may expel for any crime forbidden in the word of God, but the General conference can do no such thing, unless the crime is specified 'not *implied* in the "General Rules."

It is, then, a matter of fact that the "General Rules" did not at any period prior to 1808 comprise *all* the terms of membership in the Discipline. There is nothing in the constitution adopted at that time which intimates that thenceforth they are to be so construed. Terms of membership then existing elsewhere were continued in the Discipline, subject to the will of a majority of the General conference; notwithstanding that, the "General Rules" of Mr. Wesley were made a part of the constitution, and unalterable but by the Restrictive Rule process. The assumption, then, that "General Rules" and "terms of membership" are equivalent and convertible terms, is contrary to the facts and against the whole history of Methodist law; and the argument based upon this assumption falls to the ground.

The constitution, then, by forbidding the General conference to *revoke* or *change* the "General Rules," did not take away the power to make rules instituting new terms of membership not in conflict with any existing "General Rule;" and, therefore, admitting that a law prohibiting slaveholding would institute a new term of membership, still, for any thing contained in the fourth restriction to the contrary, the General conference is competent to pass a simple rule of Discipline which will exclude all slaveholders from the Church.

CHAPTER V.

RECAPITULATION AND AUTHORITIES.

In the foregoing argument the design has been to show the correctness of the following statements:

1. The General conference has *all* power to make "rules and regulations" for the Church, except in those particulars in which such power is *expressly* withheld by the restrictions imposed; and, therefore, the General conference is competent to make a rule excluding all slaveholders from the Church, unless the power thereto is *excepted out* of the "full powers" conferred by the sweeping terms of the grant.

2. There is no constitutional restric-

tion saying in just so many words, or in words of like import, that *the General conference shall not make a rule excluding all slaveholders from the Church;* and yet there must be some provision entirely equivalent to this, or the General conference *has* power to make such an exscinding rule.

3. The *fourth* restriction—the only one claimed as limiting the power of the General conference in the premises—in forbidding that body to *revoke* or *change* the "General Rules," does not thereby inhibit a statutory rule excluding all slaveholders from the Church, unless such rule would either repeal or modify some existing "General Rule."

4. The "General Rule" relating to slave-*buying* and slave-*selling* does *not* "authorize" slave-*holding;* and, therefore, an exscinding rule will neither

repeal nor modify the existing "General Rule" on slavery, nor in any other wise conflict with its provisions.

5. The *fourth* restriction does not take from the General conference the power to make rules prescribing in the Discipline *new* terms of membership, unless that part of the Church code known technically as the "General Rules of the United Societies" did, at the time it became a part of the paramount law of the Methodist Episcopal Church, and in the estimation of those who imposed the restriction, comprise *all* the terms of membership then in the Discipline, for the General conference was not forbidden to revoke or change other rules than those specified.

6. As a matter of fact the "General Rules of the United Societies" *never did*, and do not *now* and never *can* with

propriety comprise *all* the terms of membership in the Discipline; and, therefore, there are, and always have been, and will always continue to be terms of membership which the General conference has power to change, abolish, or re-enact at pleasure; and in so doing will not revoke nor change the "General Rules."

7. The doctrine that the General conference is forbidden to make a rule instituting in the Discipline a new term of membership, for the reason *merely* that it *is* a new one, has no foundation in the constitution of the Church, and is at variance with past history and existing facts.

8. The Church has always considered the matter of slave "buying and selling" and the matter of slaveholding as proper subjects for separate and

distinct laws. They have never been conjoined in the same Disciplinary rule. The General conference of 1808 introduced the law relating to the former into the constitution of the Church, thus putting it beyond the power of the General conference thereafter to "revoke or change" the rule forbidding members of the Church to buy or sell slaves except with a view to their emancipation; while every thing relating to *slaveholding* was *left out* of the constitution, and no restrictions were imposed upon the powers of the General conference in relation thereto, thus continuing to that body the same "full powers" over the whole subject of slaveholding as it had hitherto possessed.

9. The whole argument may be briefly summed up thus: The General

conference is competent to make a simple rule of Discipline excluding all slaveholders from the Church, unless forbidden thereto, by restrictions imposed upon the "full powers" couched in the terms of the grant; but the restrictions imposed *do not*, either in direct terms or by any fair implication, forbid the General conference to make such a rule, and, therefore, the General conference has *full* powers to make it.

In confirmation of the conclusion reached in the foregoing argument many weighty authorities might be cited, were it indeed important to refer to authorities at all on a matter so plain. I will content myself, however, with citing but one, which, coming as it does from the combined wisdom of the highest judicial tribunal of the

Church, must be at least *persuasive* if not *conclusive* on the question. It will be seen that it bears *directly* and *specifically* on the constitutional powers of the General conference in relation to slavery in its connections with the Church, and it is absolutely *demonstrative* that in the judgment of the supreme legislative and judicial council of the Church, there is no constitutional provision whatever limiting the power of the General conference over the matter of slaveholding.

In the General conference of 1844 sundry delegates from southern conferences *protested* against the action of that body in the case of Bishop Andrew. The PROTESTANTS say:

"The southern conferences, in agreeing to the main principles of the compromise law of 1804 and 1816, conceded by express stipulation their right to resist northern interference in any form upon the condition pledged by the north that, while the *whole Church*, by common consent, united in proper effort for the mitigation and final removal of slavery, the north was not to interfere, by *excluding from membership* or from ministerial office in the Church persons *owning* and *holding* slaves in states where emancipation is not practicable, and where the liberated slave is not permitted to enjoy freedom. Such was the compact of 1804 and 1816 finally agreed to by the parties after a long and fearful struggle, and such is the compact now—the proof being derived from history and from living witnesses. . . It must be seen from the manner in which the compromise was effected in the shape of law, agreed to by equal contracting parties, 'the several annual conferences,' after long and formal negotiation, that it was not a mere legislative enactment, a simple decree of the General conference, but partakes of the nature of a grave compact, and is invested with all the sacredness and sanctions of a solemn treaty, binding respectively the well-known parties to its terms and stipulations."*

These PROTESTANTS do not intimate, even by remotest innuendo, that there is any provision of either the Restrictive or General Rules which forbids the General conference to interfere with slavery by *excluding from membership* persons *owning* and *holding* slaves. Hard pressed as they were, it never occurred to them that we were *constitutionally* a slaveholding Church, nor that the constitution, either in its letter or spirit, restricted the powers of the General conference over the whole matter of slaveholding. They did claim that such a restriction existed in fact, but instead of attributing it to any provision of

*Journal of General Conference for 1844, pages 188 and 189.

the *organic* law of the Church, they declared it to have sprung from the operation of a "grave compact," a "solemn treaty," entered into and consummated in 1804 and 1816 by and between the northern and southern conferences as "equal contracting parties;" and that in pursuance of this "compact" slavery was not only tolerated by the law of the Church where emancipation was prohibited by the civil law, but that this "compact" was of such general and binding obligation as to be equivalent to a constitutional injunction. It is worthy of remark, that they do not pretend that this "compact," after giving it all the effect they claim for it, inhibits a statutory rule *excluding from membership* persons owning and holding slaves in states where emancipation is practicable, and where the liberated slave is permitted to enjoy his freedom, but the whole tenor of their claim seems to concede that in such cases there was not even a "compact" or "treaty" restraining the General conference in the premises.

The General conference appointed a committee consisting of three of the most distinguished and learned men of that body—Doctors DURBIN, PECK, and ELLIOTT—to draw up a "Reply to the Protest." The "Reply" is drawn with masterly skill, and is in all respects just such a document as one acquainted with the able chairman of that committee would have anticipated from his pen. It may be found *in extenso* in the Journal of the General Conference for the year 1844, pages 199–210.

After giving a concise statement of

the *facts* in the case of Bishop Andrew, the "Reply" goes on to say:

"Such are the facts in the case of Bishop Andrew. We now proceed to notice the law. Nearly all the objections raised in the Protest against the action of the General conference may be reduced to two; namely, that that body has violated the *constitutional* and the *statutory* law of the Church. That it has violated the constitutional law the Protest attempts to prove by representing its late action as a breach of what it calls 'the compromise law of the Church on the subject of slavery,' meaning, as is supposed, the section on slavery, particularly that paragraph which relates to traveling preachers. The entire language on this subject is evidently formed so as to make the impression on any reader not intimately acquainted with the history and Discipline of the Methodist Episcopal Church, that there has been some period—whether in 1804 or 1816 does not clearly appear from the Protest—when the question of slavery was settled in the Methodist Episcopal Church as it was in the

General Government at the adoption of the Federal Constitution—that 'the confederating annual conferences,' 'after a vexed and protracted negotiation,' met in convention, and the section on slavery 'was finally agreed to by the parties after a long and fearful struggle,' as 'a compact,' 'a treaty' which can not be altered by the General conference till certain constitutional restrictions are removed. So that now any interference on the part of that body with the question of slavery in the southern conferences, is as unconstitutional as it is admitted would be the interference of the General Government with the question in the southern states.

"After the boldness with which this doctrine is advanced, and the confidence with which it is relied upon as 'the first and principal ground occupied by the minority in this Protest,' it will be difficult for the uninitiated to believe that it is as unfounded in fact as it is ingenious in its 'legal casuistry.' It is, indeed, true that the question of slavery had been long and anxiously agitated in the Church, and the various General conferences had endeavored to adjust the matter so as to promote the greatest good of all parties; but this very fact goes to disprove the position assumed in the Protest; for as the attention of the Church had been thus strongly called to the subject, if it had been the intention to guard the question of slavery by constitutional provisions, it would have been done when the Church actually did meet to frame a constitution. But nothing of the kind appears. For when in 1808 it was resolved that the General conference, instead of consisting as before of all the traveling elders, should be a delegated body, and when it was determined that that body—unlike the General Government, which has no powers, but such as are expressly conferred—should have all powers but such as are expressly taken away—when this vast authority was about to be given to the General conference, among 'the limitations and restrictions' imposed, *there is not one word on the subject of slavery, nor was any attempt made to introduce any such restriction.* The only provision any where established by that General conference of constitutional force was the General Rule forbidding the buying and selling of human beings with an intention to enslave them. So that in direct opposition to the assertion of the Protest we maintain that the section on slavery is 'a mere legislative enactment, a simple decree of a General conference,' as much under its control as any other part of the Discipline not covered by the Restrictive Rules. If additional proof of the truth of this position were needed, it might be adduced in the fact that that section which the Protest represents to have been settled in 1804 was not only altered at the General conference or convention of 1808, but also at the delegated General conferences of 1812, 1816, 1820, and 1824. And, although the Protest speaks of it as 'usually known' by the name of 'the compromise act,' the greater part of this General conference have never heard either that appellation or that character ascribed to it till the present occasion.

"But, although this General conference can not admit that any portion of the section on slavery is constitutional in its character, and, therefore, could not under any circumstances allow the imputation of the Protest that they have violated the constitution of the Church, yet they do admit that it is *law*—law, too, which the General conference (though possessing full powers in the premises) has never altered except at the above periods, and then in each instance for the further indulgence of the south."*

This authority fairly and fully sustains the following propositions:

1. When in 1808 it was resolved that the General conference should thenceforth be a delegated body, it was also determined that this delegated General conference "*should have all powers except such as are expressly taken away.*"

2. "When this *vast authority* was about to be given to the General conference, among the limitations and restrictions imposed *there is not one word on the subject of slavery, nor was any*

*Journal of General Conference of 1844, page 203.

attempt made to introduce any such restriction."

3. The *absence* of constitutional restriction is not the result of mere *oversight*, but of *intentional omission;* "*for as the attention of the Church had been thus strongly called to the subject, if it had been the intention to guard the question of slavery by constitutional provisions, it would have been done when the Church actually did meet to frame a constitution.* BUT NOTHING OF THE KIND APPEARS."

4. The chapter on slavery, though not constitutional in its character, is, nevertheless, *law*—law in relation to *slaveholding* — a subject-matter over which the General conference "*possesses full powers in the premises.*"

5. The whole argument of the "Protest" going to prove that there is any

constitutional limitation of the powers of the General conference to make any and all rules against slavery, though "ingenious in its legal casuistry," is "*unfounded in fact.*"

In a word, the Protest maintains substantially the modern dogma that the law of the Church not only tolerates slavery, but that, under the circumstances, this toleration is tantamount to a constitutional provision to that intent; or, in other words, that the Methodist Episcopal Church is *constitutionally* a slaveholding Church, and, therefore, that any interference with slavery on the part of the General conference, by *excluding from membership* or from ministerial office persons *owning* and *holding* slaves, would be unconstitutional.

To this assumption the committee,

sustained by a very large majority of the General conference, answers, *denying flatly* that there is a single constitutional provision restricting the powers of the General conference over the matter of slavery, and *asserting* in most positive terms the *plenary* powers of the General conference in the premises.

Now, let it be observed that one point directly made in the "Protest" is that the General conference has not power to make a rule "*excluding from membership* persons *owning* and *holding* slaves," and let it be observed further that the General conference declares that it "possesses *full powers* in the premises," and it follows inevitably either that *non*-slaveholding is *now* a term of membership in the Church, or that the General conference has the power

to make it such, and either view will amply justify a statutory rule excluding all slaveholders from the Church.

Even, then, admitting that the present law of the Church does tolerate slavery, it does so simply for the reason that the supreme council of the Church, in the legitimate exercise of its functions, has not excluded it; nevertheless, the General conference, "*possessing* FULL POWERS *in the premises*," may refuse to tolerate it longer, for "among the limitations and restrictions imposed *there is not one word on the subject of slavery, nor was any attempt made to introduce any such restriction.*" *Nay, more, such a restriction was deliberately and with design omitted from the constitution.*

It is true the committee who drew up the "Reply," as well as the grave and reverend body of men who sanctioned it, were looking only for authority to pronounce sentence against Bishop Andrew for having become a slaveholder; but it is perfectly immaterial what may have been the application which they intended to make of these elementary doctrines of Methodist jurisprudence. They expounded the law in its general principles, and most plainly and fully set forth the doctrine that the General conference has *unrestricted* powers over the subject of slavery so far as its relation to the Church may be concerned. Verily, Dr. Bond well said, and he had high authority for the opinion, "THE GENERAL CONFERENCE IS COMPETENT TO PASS A SIMPLE RULE OF DISCIPLINE WHICH WILL EXCLUDE ALL SLAVEHOLDERS FROM THE CHURCH."*

* Christian Advocate and Journal, July 5, 1855.

CHAPTER VI.

PERILS OF THE MEMBERSHIP.

WHETHER the interests of the Church and its membership are in imminent peril while subject to the control of a body of ministers, constituted as is our delegated General conference and vested with such powers as are herein claimed for that body, is not *now* the question under consideration. It is an important one—one entitled to full and careful examination, and if dangers really impend, all necessary changes ought to be made to protect the interests of the Church and the rights of all parties; but such a question is in no wise involved in the present discussion. And all that has been said about the rights of our membership being "at the discretion of any possible despotism of the clergy," and that this doctrine "would leave the Church the veriest despotism known not only now in the ecclesiastical world, but in ecclesiastical history," and that "it would be a degradation for an American citizen to endure it,"* is "*ad captandum* logic"—mere rodomontade; for, admitting it all to be true, it would not even then prove that the General conference *has no such power*, but only that it *ought not to have*, and that if the constitution does so imperil the interests and rights of others, then it ought to be changed. In relation to this point it is only necessary to say

* Appeal to the Methodist Episcopal Church on Slavery, page 12.

that it is conceded on all hands that the power to make, revoke, and change Disciplinary terms of membership is at least in the hands of the ministry. A delegated General conference is that ministry *representatively* assembled in such ratio as they themselves have determined. "Discipline in our Church originates in the body of itinerant elders who are all supposed to be present by representation once in four years."* Till the entire ministry is fallen, it is not at all probable that *ambitious, irreligious,* and *designing* men, having no sense of moral and ministerial obligation to God and to his Church, will be chosen by the annual conferences to bear so high a trust. The delegates come up fresh from their constituents to do their will, and, hav-

* Bishop Hedding on Discipline, page 7.

ing fulfilled their mission, they return to them disrobed of all authority. Under such circumstances it is morally certain that whatever "rules and regulations" they may enact will be acceptable to the great body of their constituency. And not only so, but whatever rules they make relating to the deportment of the membership apply to themselves equally with other members of the Church. To such a senate of ministers I can confide my dearest and highest ecclesiastical interests, and such considerations have always given me a sense of security against any outrageous acts of legislation by the General conference.

Moreover, the man who alleges that the General conference has no power to make new terms of membership, and, of consequence, has no power to make an exscinding rule on slavery, on the ground that the possession of such a power jeopardizes the dearest *rights* of the membership, *begs* the very question in debate; for if the General conference has *power* to make the rule, then whatever the rule may require it can not by any possibility interfere with the *rights* of the membership. And for this view there is authority, which the author of the "APPEAL" ought not to gainsay. I quote from *Stevens's Church Polity*, pp. 116, 117:

"Where obedience is necessary the corresponding rights are reciprocal, but where obedience is voluntary the privileges are conditional, and are in extent *no more* than are stipulated for in the contract between those who govern and those who are governed. Now, this is precisely the relation we sustain to the Methodist Episcopal Church. It did not extend its jurisdiction over us in our infancy, nor till we voluntarily entered its pale. Our becoming members was a voluntary act, done with a previous knowledge of the rights we were required to surrender and the privileges we acquired by the contract. We could not carry with us into this voluntary association any natural rights incompatible with the contract we entered into. . . The rights which a Methodist possesses as such are purely conventional. They are not natural, but acquired rights, and they are determined by the articles of association contained in the book of Discipline. *The Church is a voluntary association entered into for religious purposes.* Whoever enters its communion is entitled to all the immunities which the articles of association hold out to him and *no more.* If he finds upon experiment that the religious advantages he acquires do not compensate him for the sacrifices he is required to make, he has an indefeasible right to withdraw from the community, but he has no right to demand of the Church to change her economy for his accommodation."*

* For a fuller statement of the same doctrine see Bond's "Economy of Methodism," pages 26, 27, 28.

www.ingramcontent.com/pod-product-compliance
Lightning Source LLC
LaVergne TN
LVHW021406110826
845150LV00007B/1810

* 9 7 8 1 4 2 5 5 1 1 8 2 1 *